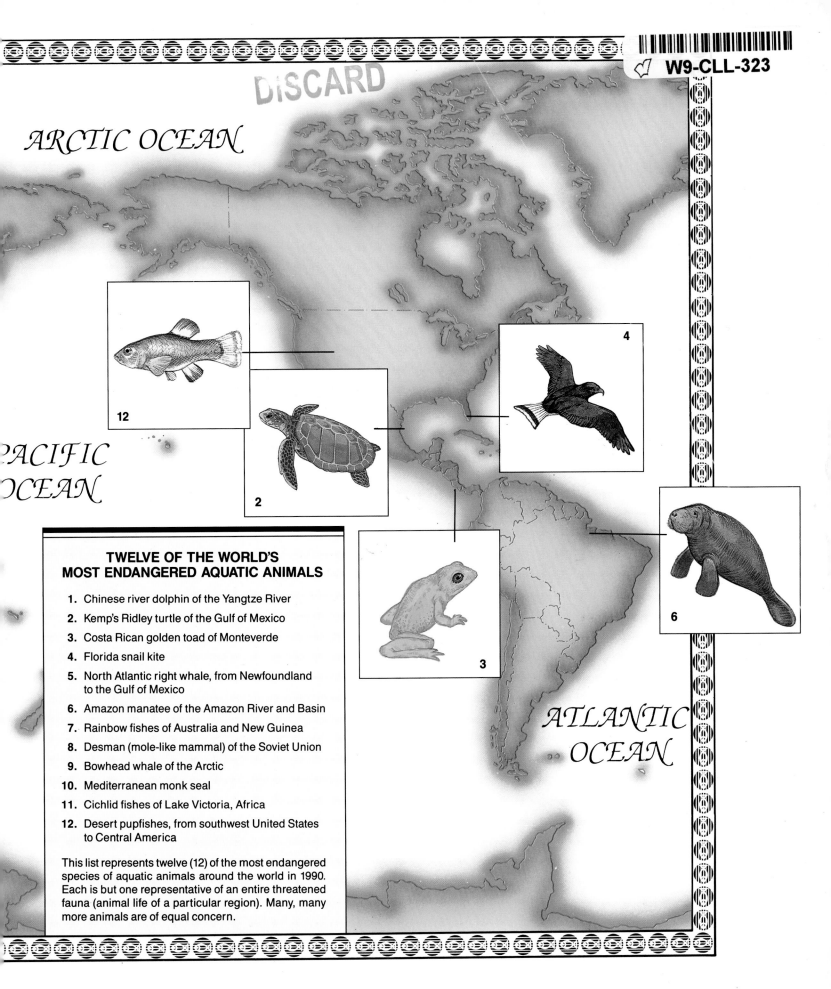

ARCTIC OCEAN

PACIFIC OCEAN

ATLANTIC OCEAN

12

2

4

6

3

TWELVE OF THE WORLD'S MOST ENDANGERED AQUATIC ANIMALS

1. Chinese river dolphin of the Yangtze River
2. Kemp's Ridley turtle of the Gulf of Mexico
3. Costa Rican golden toad of Monteverde
4. Florida snail kite
5. North Atlantic right whale, from Newfoundland to the Gulf of Mexico
6. Amazon manatee of the Amazon River and Basin
7. Rainbow fishes of Australia and New Guinea
8. Desman (mole-like mammal) of the Soviet Union
9. Bowhead whale of the Arctic
10. Mediterranean monk seal
11. Cichlid fishes of Lake Victoria, Africa
12. Desert pupfishes, from southwest United States to Central America

This list represents twelve (12) of the most endangered species of aquatic animals around the world in 1990. Each is but one representative of an entire threatened fauna (animal life of a particular region). Many, many more animals are of equal concern.

DO FISHES GET THIRSTY?

Questions Answered
by Dr. Les Kaufman
and the Staff of the
New England Aquarium

Franklin Watts
New York | London | Toronto | Sydney
A New England Aquarium Book
1991

Diagrams by James Needham

Photographs copyright ©: New England Aquarium: pp. 1, 5, 10 top
(all Bill Wasserman), 7, 16, 23, 28 (all Paul Erickson), 9 left
(Catherine Paladino), 25 (Scott Kraus), 26, 35 (both Macy Lawrence),
27 right (Chris Newbert), 32 (Patricia Fiorelli), 34 (Richard Duggan);
Loren McIntyre: pp. 8, 19 right; Marty Snyderman: p. 9 right;
Photo Researchers Inc.: pp. 10 bottom (Charlie Ott), 11 left
(Steinhart Aquarium/Tom McHugh); Bruce Coleman Inc.: pp. 11 right
(Jane Burton), 22 (Ron & Valerie Taylor); Animals Animals: pp. 12,
15 (both Zig Leszczynski), 13 left (Breck P. Kent), 29 (OSF/Peter Parks),
30 (OSF/G.I. Bernard), 31 (Tim Rock); Kenneth R.H. Read: pp. 13
both right, 21 bottom; Raymond Hixon: p. 17; Fred Bavendam: pp. 18,
19 left; Andrew Martinez: pp. 20 left, 21 top, 27 left; Jeff Rotman:
p. 20 right; Dennis Stierer: p. 33.

Library of Congress Cataloging-in-Publication Data

Do fishes get thirsty? / questions answered by Dr. Les Kaufman and
staff of the New England Aquarium.
p. cm.
Includes bibliographical references and index.
Summary: Explains, using a question-and-answer format, the
differences between several fish and other aquatic species.
ISBN 0-531-10992-5 (lib. bdg.).—ISBN 0-531-15214-6
1. Fishes—Miscellanea—Juvenile literature. 2. Aquatic animals—
Miscellanea—Juvenile literature. 3. Aquariums, Public—
Miscellanea—Juvenile literature. [1. Fishes—Miscellanea.
2. Aquatic animals—Miscellanea. 3. Questions and answers.]
I. Kaufman, Les. II. New England Aquarium Corporation.
QL617.2D6 1991
597—dc20   90-46871 CIP AC

Contents:

Acknowledgments

The questions and answers in this book reflect the ideas of many of us at the New England Aquarium, but we are especially indebted to Dr. Les Kaufman, former Curator of Education at the New England Aquarium, and now Chief Scientist and head of the Aquarium's Edgerton Research Laboratory. We wish also to thank Dr. Paul Boyle, Director of Programs and Exhibits and acting Curator of Education, as well as education staff members—Terry Martin, Carol Fiore, Berit Solstad, Alan Anderson, Tanya Gregoire, Pat Pittman,—and members of the Curatorial Department for helping shape the answers here; and the two primary writers, Catherine Paladino and Ken Mallory. Finally, we would like to thank the Aquarium's Director of Marketing, Cynthia Mackey, and the Associate Director of Public Relations and Media Programs, Sandra Goldfarb, for their guiding support in making this and other books like it a reality.

Introduction: Why Do We Need Public Aquariums?

Fish or Fishes: How Are These Terms Used? Use "fish" when referring to one species (10 salmon are 10 fish). Use "fishes" when referring to more than one species (10 salmon, 3 trout, and 1 codfish are 14 fishes).

To care for something—whether it is a person, an animal, or anything at all—is to familiarize ourselves with it. And if we care for something, we are willing to try to preserve it. As people who live on the land, most of us know very little about what goes on beneath the other three-quarters of the Earth—the waters of our oceans, lakes, and ponds. An aquarium is one of the rare places where we can encounter this strange, vast world and make it familiar.

Aquariums are observatories for the marvelous creatures of the aquatic world. They not only open windows for us, they allow scientists to study underwater life closely as well. Through what they discover in the aquarium setting, scientists can unlock secrets of nature, and then share that knowledge with all of us.

Most of the questions in this book are questions of "what" and "where." They are called descriptive questions, because the answers describe what there is to see, hear, or smell in the world. After you have learned to describe, you are ready to ask more exciting questions—"how" do things come to be as they are, and "when." This is what science is all about. Everyone wonders "why," but even scientists can't always answer that kind of question for you. "Why?" is a question you must answer for yourself.

Young nature fans marvel at the New England Aquarium's newest exhibit about sea stars.

What Is a Fish?

A fish is a cold-blooded animal with a backbone. It usually lives in water, absorbs oxygen from the water with *gills*, and swims with 7 fins. But some fishes don't quite fit this general description. Electric eels are fishes. But they only have fins along their stomach, small pectoral (side) fins, and they can breathe oxygen from the air.

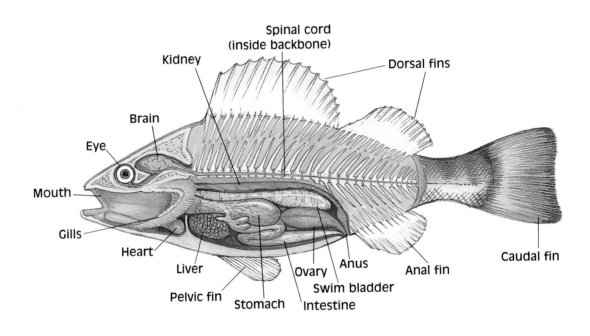

Spinal cord
(inside backbone)

Kidney

Dorsal fins

Brain

Eye

Mouth

Gills

Heart

Liver

Pelvic fin

Stomach

Ovary

Intestine

Swim bladder

Anus

Anal fin

Caudal fin

ANATOMY OF A FISH

How Many Different Kinds of Fishes Are There?

Over 30,000 different kinds or species of fishes live in the world today. And scientists are discovering new ones all the time. To help organize this growing list, we use a scientific naming system. Of the species discovered so far, only about two-thirds have names. It takes time to learn enough about each one—its looks and habits—to recognize that it is unique and should have a name of its own. Some species are so alike that scientists have to count rows of scales or teeth to tell species apart.

The fishes in the New
England Aquarium's giant
ocean tank mirror the
diversity of fishes on a
Caribbean coral reef.

The pirarucú from the Amazon River was once one of the world's largest freshwater fishes. Over-fishing has made them much harder to find.

What Is the Smallest Fish?

Several kinds of gobies are candidates for the smallest fish award. They are the freshwater Pygmy and Luzon gobies of the Philippines, and the saltwater Marshall Islands goby (GO-bee) of the South Pacific. Another candidate is the tiny rice fish from Thailand. All reach a maximum length of about a half inch (1.3 centimeters), roughly the size of a grain of rice.

What Is the Biggest Fish?

The biggest fish in the world is a gentle shark, the giant whale shark. This colossal fish grows to be the length of two school buses, or about 60 feet (18.3 meters). Weighing over 25 tons (22,680 kilograms), the whale shark eats only tiny creatures like animal plankton, small fish, and squid. Its throat is too small to swallow anything much bigger than a softball. Whale sharks are beautiful and usually harmless to humans.

In fresh water, one of the largest fishes is the pirarucú. This South American river fish can grow up to 15 feet long (4.6 meters). But pirarucú are not as big as they used to be. Hunters too often kill them for food before they are full grown. Pirarucú make good targets for spear fishermen, as they surface about every 10 to 20 minutes for air. Since the largest ones have been killed off, most pirarucú are now only 6 to 7 feet (about 2 meters) long.

(Below right) Fifty feet (15 m) long and weighing 40,000 pounds (18,000 kg), the whale shark is the world's largest fish. Scuba divers are dwarfed by its presence.

(Below left) Besides gobies, the rice fish from Thailand shown here are counted among the world's smallest fishes. They are about half an inch (12.7 mm) long.

Fishes depend on special places such as mangrove swamps to breed and raise their young.

Fishes depend on special places such as mangrove swamps to breed and raise their young.

Where Do Fishes Live?

(Below) A pupfish from Death Valley National Monument lives in waters as hot as a volcanic spring.

Fishes live almost anywhere that is wet. Since water covers 75 percent of our planet, fishes live all over the globe. They're found in lakes at the tops of mountains and in oceanic trenches nearly seven miles (11 kilometers) deep. Fishes can thrive in shallows only inches deep. Some, like a few *killifishes,* will even live in a footprint. The killifish's brief life begins and ends in the time it takes for a puddle to dry up.

Fishes are cold-blooded, but that doesn't always mean their blood is cold. Most simply assume the same temperature as their surroundings. For the ice fish this can be as cold as the Antarctic Sea—below freezing. For the desert pupfish, this can be as hot as a volcanic spring—120 degrees Fahrenheit (48.9 degrees C).

Whether it is a clear, rushing stream or a still, murky swamp, nearly any body of water is home to some type of fish. With such diversity of environments to occupy, it's no wonder fishes have become the world's largest group of backboned animals.

Are Fishes Good Parents?

Most fishes release a gigantic number of eggs that survive on their own, or they put lots of energy into caring for a few. The codfish produces literally millions of eggs. The California surf perch does not give birth to her twenty or so young until they're practically adults.

Between these extremes are many variations. Freshwater fishes called mouthbrooders hold their fertilized eggs in their mouths like cough drops. When the babies hatch, the parent spits them out to let them feed, then gathers them back in at the first sign of danger.

Few fishes show the ingenuity of the South American *cichlid* called the *acara.* It lays its eggs on a leaf, then pushes its floating baby carriage around until the young are safely hatched. Even after the babies are born, the parent drags the young around on the leaf to find good and safe places for them to feed.

(Below left) A male cichlid guards its young

(Below right) Cichlid fishes from Africa use their mouths for both incubating their eggs and providing a refuge for developing young.

Can a Fish Live Out of Water?

Fishes suffocate if they're kept out of water too long. But mudskippers and lungfishes are exceptions. Mudskippers spend more time skittering about on tropical mud flats than they do swimming underwater.

Most fishes only use gills for extracting oxygen from the water. But mudskippers can also use their gills to breathe air while on land. Like our lungs, gills must be kept moist to work. Mudskippers carry a portable water supply in their gill chambers when they leave the water. They add extra oxygen to it by gulping air and mixing it with the water. They can also breathe through the pores of their wet skin.

Lungfishes can live out of water for several years. Sensing a change in temperature and availability of water, the African lungfish survives dry spells by secreting a mucus cocoon and burrowing itself under sunbaked earth. It takes in air with its lung through a built-in breathing tube that leads to the surface. Even when water returns, African lungfishes must be able to breathe air or they will drown.

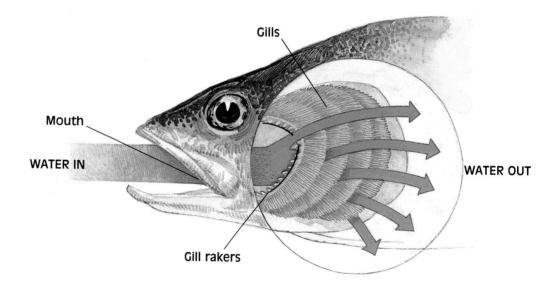

Gills

Mouth

WATER IN

WATER OUT

Gill rakers

Mudskippers can clamber about out of water by keeping their gills wet and breathing air through their wet skin.

Most fishes use gills to breathe. When a fish breathes it opens its mouth and closes it again once it draws in water. This motion forces a continuous stream of water to pass over the gills. The water brings in oxygen, which is absorbed by blood flowing through the blood vessels in the gills. Carbon dioxide is carried out by the water released through the gills.

How Well Do Fishes See?

Fishes use their eyes in much the same way we do, and sometimes their vision is just as good. In clear, brightly lit waters, fishes rely on keen eyesight to catch their food, avoid enemies, and recognize their own kind. Coral reef wrasses use sharp daytime vision to recognize other fellow wrasses by the color and pattern of their stripes. But fishes with good daylight vision don't see as well in dim light. Twilight is the time for fish-eating predators like sharks and jacks. Though they only see grainy images, their large, sensitive eyes easily pick out the form and movements of potential prey.

Some fishes that live in the pitch dark of caves or the deep sea have small eyes or none at all. Blind deep-sea rays and cave fishes rely on other senses for getting around. Lantern-eye fishes have built in "flashlights" under their eyes. These light organs contain luminescent or glow-in-the-dark bacteria. Deep-sea fishes that glow or eat glowing prey have huge eyes to see other ghostly images around them.

(Below left) A blind cavefish from Mexico can find its way around perfectly by using other senses besides sight.

(Below right) The "eyes" have it. The seeing organs of a goosefish (top) and a toadfish (bottom) help them survive life on the ocean floor in waters of the Gulf of Maine.

Do Fishes Have Ears?

Even though they have no external ears, fishes hear much the same way we do. They use internal ears to detect underwater sounds. Sound passing through a fish's head resonates in the inner ear capsules. These capsules contain liquid and several small calcified stones called *otoliths*. Sensitive hairs around the otoliths pick up vibrations, and a corresponding signal is sent to the fish's brain.

Most of the sounds a fish hears are the low booms, croaks, clicks, and grunts that other fishes make. It hears very well in this low-pitched range. But most fishes have less than a tenth of the hearing range of humans.

Goldfish, minnows, and catfish have a broader hearing range than other fishes because they have an extra hearing structure. Called the *Weberian ossicles*, this set of small bones works like the three bones in the human inner ear. For some fishes, a sound first vibrates their *swim bladders*, which are organs that help fishes to sink or float. Then the ossicles transfer these sounds so they are heard by the inner ear.

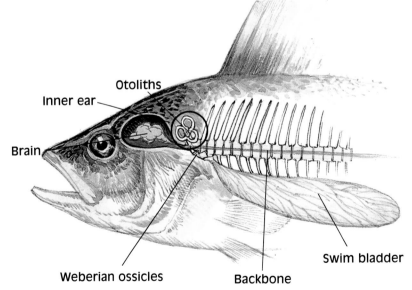

A fish hears when otoliths, a series of bone-like structures located in its inner ear, pick up sound waves transmitted from the water or the vibrating air bladder. In some fishes these sound waves are transmitted by the ossicle chain that connects the swim bladder to the inner ear. These otoliths act like the bones of our middle ear to translate sound to the brain.

A spotted drumfish lives up to its name by vibrating its swim bladder to produce the sound of a drum.

Can Fishes Talk?

Fishes talk, but they don't use language and grammar the way we do. Fishes use a variety of low-pitched sounds to convey messages to each other. They make the sort of noises that could haunt a house. Fishes moan, grunt, croak, boom, hiss, whistle, creak, shriek, and wail. They rattle their bones and gnash their teeth.

Fishes have no vocal chords. Other parts of their bodies act as noisemakers. Drumfishes make drumming sounds by vibrating muscles against their swim bladders. Giant ocean sunfishes rub teeth in their throat together to grunt like pigs.

Depending on the situation, one noisy fish could be saying "stay away," or "I'm looking for a mate," or "I'm going to eat you," or even "I'm not sure what to do next."

15

By gathering in such numbers, fish schools employ hundreds of eyes for locating food and avoiding predators.

(Facing page) When a school changes direction, it looks as though all the fish are moving in unison. Actually, they move in a wave. As soon as a fish detects that its neighbor in front or to the side has changed direction, it follows suit. In a school of fish, there is no leader.

Do Fishes Go to School?

Fish schools have nothing to do with classrooms. Fishes form schools, or groups, for protection. Schools containing millions of nearly identical fish can confuse predators. It's hard for them to pick one fish out of the crowd. If you have ever tried to keep your eye on a single snowflake in a blizzard, you know how difficult it can be.

Schooling also makes it easier for fishes to find food. When one fish in a school goes after a meal, all the rest join in.

Each fish in a school keeps a rigid distance from its neighbors. Fishes use their eyes and something called a *lateral line* sense to hold their places in the school. The lateral line is a row of pores running along the fish's sides from head to tail. Special hairs in the pores sense changes in water pressure from the movements of other fish or predators.

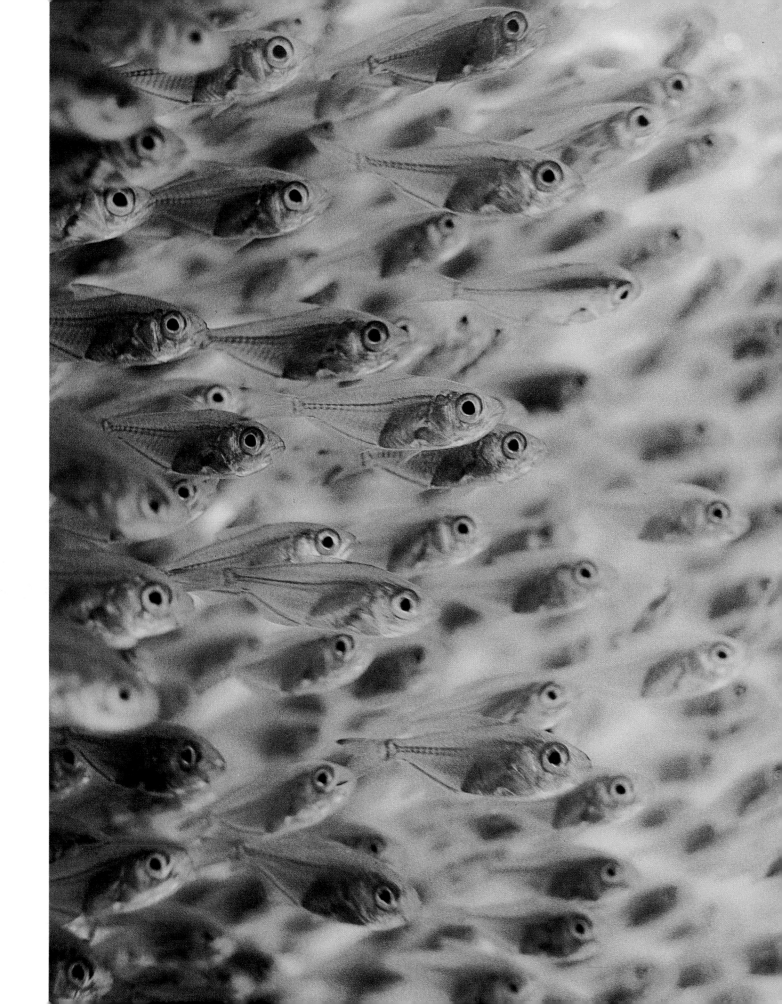

How Do Fishes Catch Their Food?

Fishes use their jaws the same way other animals use their hands or fingers. Since their jaws are not attached to their skulls, special bones allow many fishes to shoot their mouths forward like a spring to engulf their startled prey.

Another advantage for fishes is an ability to suck water in and out of their mouths. Using a partial vacuum they create in their mouth and gill chamber to draw water in, they then expel little jets of water to turn objects in mid-water or on the seafloor. A trigger fish, for example, can turn a spiny sea urchin upside down to expose its soft underbelly.

Other fish use more exotic hunting methods. Electric eels and electric rays stun their prey, sometimes with enough electricity to kill a horse. Some fishes even use tricks to get a meal. A cichlid from East Africa's Lake Malawi rolls over on its side and plays dead. If a curious fish comes in too close to investigate, the apparently dead cichlid becomes very much alive and eats the inquisitive fish.

Tuna, bluefish, and mackerel fishes hunt like a pack of wolves. First they circle a school of fishes. Then one of the hunters fires through the school, like a bowling ball into the pins. Forced out of their protective school, individual fishes are picked off with relative ease.

(Facing page) A goosefish in the Gulf of Maine opens its huge mouth, displaying the built-in lure it uses to attract, then consume, inquisitive fishes.

(Below left) The leaflike lure of the goosefish can be waved back and forth to attract prey.

(Below right) The electric eel goes fishing with a current of electricity that surrounds its body.

Do Fishes Sleep?

Fish sleep a little differently from you or me. Unlike people, fishes can't close their eyes when they sleep. They don't have eyelids. A sleeping fish is probably in more of a trance-like state than a deep sleep.

To avoid being eaten by hungry predators, fishes tuck themselves into hiding places when they nap. Some fishes swim during the day, others at night. They're like factory workers on different shifts. When the shifts change over at dawn and dusk, predators search for unwary stragglers. Daytime fishes don't see well in twilight and must scurry for cover to avoid being eaten.

The nooks and crannies of a coral reef provide fishes with lots of secret places to slumber. Parrotfishes sleep under coral reef ledges at night. They surround themselves with mucous cocoons, like sleeping bags. This masks their scent from predators like the moray eel. Triggerfishes, also night sleepers, lock themselves into holes in the coral with a strong "trigger" spine.

(Below left) A parrotfish rests for the night in the cavity of a coral reef sponge.

(Below right) Parrotfish sleep in a mucous cocoon, which they secrete each night when they settle down to rest. The cocoon helps disguise them from predators.

(Right) Scorpionfishes live up to their name with an assortment of venomous spines.

(Below) Threatened by a much larger animal breathing bubbles, a pufferfish inflates itself up like a balloon.

How Do Fishes Defend Themselves?

Most fishes hide or use camouflage to protect themselves from hungry predators. This is especially true when fishes are young and vulnerable. Baby sling-jaw wrasses and baby batfish, for example, live in mangrove swamps and resemble the dead leaves of mangrove trees. When they are ready to become adults, they join up with a leaf or two and then float out over their new coral reef home. There they can hide in the reef's crannies and take on their normal adult colors and shapes.

Fishes have an amazing assortment of defenses. Pufferfish inflate like a balloon to become too large to swallow. Lionfish, stonefish, and coral catfish are only some of the fishes that have venomous spines. Some fishes can produce an electric shock. Still others release deadly chemicals into the water. The Moses sole, a flounder from the Red Sea, releases milky poison so powerful that even sharks swim away, shaking their heads.

Are Sharks Really Vicious?

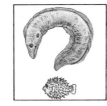

Sharks get a lot of bad publicity that they don't always deserve. But sometimes they do. If you decide to go swimming off a seal haul-out area on the northern California coast, there's a possibility that a great white shark might mistake you for a seal, one of its favorite foods. White sharks and other so-called man-eaters are powerful, finely tuned eating machines. If you are in the wrong place at the wrong time, you could end up being a meal.

But there are over 350 kinds of sharks in the world, and most of them don't bother people. There are slightly over a foot-long (.3 meter) cookie cutter sharks that scoop bites the size of an ice cream scoop from unsuspecting whales, tunas, and porpoises. Then there are basking sharks, nearly 40 foot-long (13-meter) giants whose idea of a good meal is to filter the plankton soup that floats in the water around them.

Sharks deserve our respect and wonder. And for all their bad reputation for taking lives, sharks may someday be better known for saving them instead. Their ability to resist disease has long attracted medical researchers. Substances from their *cartilage* may someday provide drugs against cancer. Their ability to resist disease may even provide clues for a cure for AIDS.

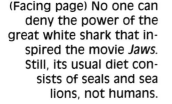

(Facing page) No one can deny the power of the great white shark that inspired the movie *Jaws*. Still, its usual diet consists of seals and sea lions, not humans.

(Below) The ragged teeth of a sand tiger shark give it a frightening appearance, but like more than 350 other kinds of sharks, sand tigers are sometimes given a bad reputation they don't deserve.

Do Fishes Get Thirsty?

Saltwater fishes need to drink a lot more than freshwater fishes do. Water flows in and out of a fish's body through a process called *osmosis*. In osmosis, water moves from where there is less dissolved salt to where there is more. Since seawater is saltier than the liquids in a fish's body, water inside the fish is constantly flowing out.

If they didn't drink to replace the lost water, saltwater fishes would dry up like prunes. But seawater is so salty, a fish could get sick drinking it. Special cells in the ocean fish's gills rid the body of some salt. Its digestive tracts remove the rest.

Freshwater fishes have the opposite problem. Liquids in their bodies are saltier than fresh water. So water flows into their bodies constantly. To keep from getting water-logged, freshwater fishes "bail" themselves out. They pass large amounts of water from their bodies as dilute urine.

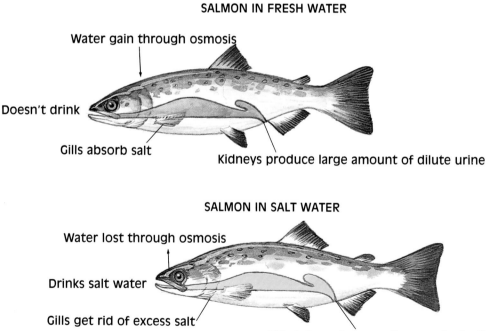

SALMON IN FRESH WATER

Water gain through osmosis

Doesn't drink

Gills absorb salt

Kidneys produce large amount of dilute urine

SALMON IN SALT WATER

Water lost through osmosis

Drinks salt water

Gills get rid of excess salt

Kidneys produce small amount of salty urine

The salmon shown here are good models for how osmosis works because they spend part of their lives in fresh and part in salt water.

Source: *An Introduction to the Biology of Marine Life*, Second Edition, by James L. Sumich (Dubuque, Iowa: William C. Brown Company Publishers), p. 13 © 1980.

What Is a Right Whale?

A right whale is the wrong kind of whale to be if you are living in the ocean today. This is especially true for the North Atlantic right whale, whose population may be as few as 300 whales. Whales are mammals, like humans. They breathe air with lungs, bear living young and provide them with milk from mammary glands, and they are warm-blooded. Unlike dolphins, which are toothed whales, the right whale filters flealike *copepods* with a structure called a *baleen* plate that looks like a big moustache on the inside of its mouth.

Right whales were easy targets for whale hunters because they swim slowly at the surface. Since discovering a summer population off Nova Scotia's Bay of Fundy in 1980, the New England Aquarium has taken a special interest in the North Atlantic right whale. Research detective work by Aquarium staff and other whale researchers has uncovered a winter breeding ground off the coast of Georgia. Other right whales winter off Cape Cod. But where most of the population lives is still a mystery.

(Below left) New England Aquarium researchers watch as several North Atlantic right whales mill at the water's surface.

(Below right) Sometimes right whales poke their heads out of the water, probably just to get a look around. This behavior somewhat resembles a submarine's use of a periscope.

Everyone loves sea stars, except the clams and other sea animals they choose to seize and devour.

What Is an Invertebrate?

(Above left) Some corals hide in limestone houses during the day, emerging at night to feed.

(Above right) Some of the tropical ocean's most important invertebrates are the millions of coral animals that make up a coral reef. Some colonies of corals make formations in the shape of giant elkhorns, as shown here with a scuba diver hovering above.

Most of the animals in the world are invertebrates, or animals without backbones. Compared with them, we vertebrates are the odd ones out. There are well over 30 million kinds of invertebrates on Earth. Only one out of a thousand species is a vertebrate.

Even though they may be spineless, invertebrates have their own special support structures. The shell of a clam, a snail, or a lobster provides support and protection. One of the most important invertebrates in the ocean world is the tiny animal called a coral *polyp*. Millions of them build the largest natural structures on Earth, the coral reef. A polyp is similar to a jellyfish but it stays in one place. Each polyp sits in a hard, cuplike skeleton that it forms by converting the calcium in seawater into solid limestone.

(Facing page) The moray eel has an undeserved reputation as a sea monster. It is usually a reclusive creature, hiding in underwater caves until night.

The frightening image of a glowing deep-sea viper fish would fit just about anyone's idea of a sea monster.

Are There Really Any Sea Monsters?

Of course there are sea monsters! There are some wild-looking creatures in the sea, and some enormous ones. There are sharks over 45 feet (13.7 meters) long. There are deep-sea vipers, hatchets, and dragonfishes. There is a red-lipped worm the length of a man, and it lives in hot lava vents at the bottom of the sea. And there are deep-sea giant squid 65 feet (19.8 meters) long.

As for any undiscovered large animals on the scale of the dinosaurs, scientists were given new hope with the discovery of the "megamouth." This 15- to 20-foot-(4.6- to 6.1-meter) long shark managed to escape our attention until it accidentally swallowed a U.S. Navy sea anchor off Hawaii in 1976. It has a large mouth that glows in the dark, thanks to fireflylike bioluminescent bacteria. The glow probably lures food on a one-way trip into the megamouth's cavernous stomach.

Is there a Loch Ness Monster, or a dinosaur called Mikele Mbembe in the People's Republic of the Congo, or a giant sea serpent? Perhaps—we simply don't know.

What Was the First Fish?

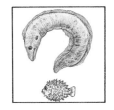

The first animal that looked something like a fish looked like the modern *amphioxis*, also known as a *lancelet*. Lancelets were alive as many as 570 million years ago, and they're still around today, living in warm, shallow seas. But instead of a backbone for support, they have a flexible skeletal rod called a *notochord*.

The first backboned creatures that resembled fishes were the early *jawless fishes*. That was about 480 million years ago. Next came fishes with jaws. Some of them had backbones of cartilage (the same substance that is at the tip of your nose) instead of bone, and were ancestors of today's sharks and rays. But the first *bony fishes*—fishes with jaws, a bony skeleton, and backbone—didn't appear until about 350 million years ago.

There are three basic models of bony fishes. The first and most primitive—the Model T Ford of fish evolution—had a simple jaw structure, which could move up and down to bite. Today's African fishes called *bichirs* are examples of these "Model T's." The heavily armored *gar* and *bowfin* are all that are left of the next wave of fishes, followed at last by true bony fishes, the most numerous backboned animals on Earth today. Many modern bony fishes have complex, extendable jaws, and an extra set of jaws for crushing food in the throat.

This lancelet, or amphioxis, is a modern-day descendant of a fish that lived 750 million years ago.

Through a process similar to breeding live-stock on a farm, fisher-men on the island of Guam (in the Pacific Ocean) feed, then capture a kind of edible shrimp called prawn.

What Is Aquaculture?

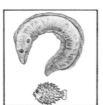

Aquaculture is the industry of farming the waters of the world. It ranges from raising algae in test tubes to ranching tuna in the open ocean.

Many countries grow aquaculture products for food. Shrimp sold in supermarkets may have been raised in pens in the Gulf of Mexico. Mussels served in restaurants may come from mussel farms on the Maine coast.

Farmers in the southern United States turned to aquaculture when they began losing money on soybean crops. They dug ponds for raising channel catfish. Catfish fillets are now a popular food among North Americans. Tilapia is a good pan fish raised for protein all over the tropics, especially in Africa and Asia. In tropical places like Jamaica, seaweed is raised for a valuable substance called algin. Algin helps give food like ice cream and salad dressings their thickness. It is also used in making paints, medicines, and cosmetics.

We also use aquaculture to raise fish for sport fishing. Overfished lakes and streams are restocked with trout raised on fish farms.

Why Do Some Ocean Animals Come Up on the Beach?

Most of the time, marine animals come up on the beach for understandable reasons. Many animals find safety in the sand, away from the many predators in the sea. Masses of horseshoe crabs, grunion fish, and turtles invade the beaches every year to breed and lay their eggs. Crocodiles come ashore to catch the heat of the sun's rays.

Why Do Other Animals Get Stranded on the Beach?

Sometimes sea animals beach themselves by mistake. Sea stars, for example, get caught too high above the high water mark and are left by the falling tide.

Whales make mistakes too, although we expect more from them because of their large-sized brain. If a herd of sociable pilot whales gets too excited chasing their favorite food, squid, they may not notice the spits of sand or beach until it's too late. If there is an onshore wind, if the tide is especially high, and there is a powerful storm, whales may strand by mistake. No one knows all the reasons why whales strand.

Stranding: How can we help?
The most important thing to understand about whale stranding is that dragging a whale back out to sea once it has stranded may cause the whale to suffer terribly. Once a whale has beached, it is in serious trouble. Interfering with a beached whale is also against the Marine Mammal Protection Act law. The best thing to do is notify the many stranding networks that are trained to deal with these emergencies. They are best able to make the tough deicision of whether or not an animal can be saved.

What Is Extinction and Why Should We Care?

Extinction means the total destruction of a kind of plant or animal. An extinct life-form will never appear again, on Earth or anywhere else. Extinctions have been occurring naturally over the history of life in Earth. A lake may have a kind of fish found nowhere else, and the lake may dry up. But many of the extinctions that occur today are caused by people, not by the rest of nature. We rip up the earth, build shopping malls, cut down forests, and catch too many fish in the sea.

The first and obvious reason we should care if fish become extinct is that we eat them. And it's not just the big, protein-rich fish we should worry about losing. Big fish eat little fish, and all sizes of fish depend on the quality of the environment they are living in. In this sense, protecting fish in the sea is as important as protecting fields of corn or wheat on land.

Fishes and other water animals have a great deal to teach us about biology and medicine. They can unlock mysteries about the evolution of life in our oceans, lakes, and streams. Besides that, watching fishes can be a lot of fun!

As the forests of the Amazon are burned down, Amazon river fishes lose the source of seeds and fruits they depend on when the river floods the forest. The flooded forest exhibit at the New England Aquarium tells this story of threatened wildlife.

What Can Aquariums Do to Protect Endangered Animals?

Public aquariums can function somewhat like a Noah's Ark. They can provide important temporary shelter for endangered animals. But the reason many of these animals became endangered in the first place is that their *habitats* were polluted or destroyed. Oil spills, household sewage, industrial wastes, overfishing, and real estate development are often the culprits. If habitats become protected, aquariums can reintroduce surviving animals to build a new population in the wild.

The New England Aquarium is a pioneer in helping endangered fishes. It is breeding desert hole pupfishes that come from Nevada's Death Valley National Monument. It helps maintain families of Appalachian (Tennessee) stream fishes. It is a shelter for Africa's Lake Victoria cichlid fishes, which were nearly wiped out by a fish-eating predator called the Nile perch. And together with the National Marine Fisheries Service, the Aquarium is creating a new endangered species list for marine fishes. This will help lawmakers to write laws to conserve coral reefs, sea grass beds, mangrove forests, and other habitats.

The New England Aquarium is one of several public aquariums worldwide with programs to assist endangered aquatic animals. The Monterey Aquarium in California is noteworthy for their work with deep sea animals and sharks. The new Chattanooga Aquarium in Tennessee has special programs for river fishes. The Townsville Aquarium in Australia features conservation of coral reef fishes. By taking an active role in preserving planet Earth and its plant and animal life, many aquariums hope to encourage their visitors to join in this cause as well.

Fishes in Boston Harbor have to survive city sewage and ocean pollution. Aquarium exhibits can show visitors how their efforts can help clean up the harbor.

Although the painted turtle shown here is not an endangered species, exhibits on the plight of turtles may someday help save the many sea turtles that are endangered.

Glossary

acara (ah-KAR-ah)—a group of freshwater cichlid fishes from South America

amphioxus (am-FEE-ox-us) See lancelet.

baleen (buh-LEEN)—the tough, flexible material that hangs in strips from the upper jaw of some whales, used for filtering fishes and plankton from the sea

bichir (BIKE-er)—primitive African freshwater fish with a long, thin body and flaglike dorsal finlets. Its air bladder works as a lung to breathe air.

bioluminescent (By-oh-LOO-muh-NES-ent)—light produced by living organisms

bony fishes—fishes that have jaws and skeletons made up primarily of bone rather than cartilage. Over 90 percent of all fishes are bony fishes.

bowfin (BOH-fin)—primitive eastern North American freshwater fish that lives in weedy areas at edges of lakes and streams. It can breathe air using its air bladder, and guards its young ferociously.

cartilage (KART-ul-ij)—tough but flexible elastic tissue that can form part or all of an animal's skeleton

cichlid (SIK-lid)—any of a large family of freshwater, spiny-finned fishes native to tropical America, India, and the Middle East. Many species are popular in home aquariums, others are food fishes.

copepod (KO-puh-pod)—any of a large family of tiny freshwater and saltwater crustaceans, invertebrates with hard shells and jointed bodies and appendages.

dorsal (DOOR-sul)—located on or near the back of an animal

gar—primitive North American freshwater fish with a long, narrow body; armored scales; and very long, beaklike jaws with needle teeth

gills—feathery organs on both sides of the head or body of fishes and aquatic invertebrates. Gills absorb oxygen from water and remove carbon dioxide from the blood.

habitat—the place, or kind of place where a plant or animal naturally lives and grows

invertebrate (in-VERT-uh-brate)—an animal without a backbone, such as a jellyfish, lobster, or insect

jawless fishes—fishes with large, sucking mouths and no jaws. They include hagfishes, lampreys, and many extinct forms.

killifish (KIL-i-fish)—a family of generally small fishes, including the desert pupfish

lancelet (LAN-slit)—fishlike ancestor of back-boned animals, having a simple body with a notochord; also called amphioxus and still alive today

lateral line—system of tiny holes (pores) running along both sides of a fish's body that enable it to detect movement in the water

notochord (NOTE-ah-kord)—a flexible skeletal rod surrounded by a tough covering that helps support the body and was the forerunner of the backbone, or vertebral column

osmosis (AHZ-mo-sus)—movement of water through a membrane from a less concentrated solution into a more concentrated one

otoliths (OHT-uhl-iths)—small calcified stones in a fish's inner ears, used in hearing and balance

polyp (POL-up)—stage in the lives of jellyfishes, sea anemones, and corals consisting of a simple stomach with a mouth surrounded by tentacles

swim bladder—a gas-filled sac beneath a fish's backbone that helps it to rise or sink and, in some fishes, aids in hearing and making sounds; also called the gas or air bladder

Weberian ossicles (web-AIR-ee-en AHS-sik-uls)—a set of small bones in some fishes that connects the swim bladder to the inner ear

Bibliography

1. The material on fishes is developed from Q. Bone and N.B Marshall, illustrated by Q. Bone, *Biology of Fishes* (Glasgow: Blackie: New York: Distributed in the United States by Routledge, Chapman and Hall, 1982); E. Clark, "Sharks: Magnificent and Misunderstood," (Washington D.C.: National Geographic Magazine, vol. 160, No. 2, August 1981) 142–186; B. Curtis, *The Life Story of the Fish: His Manners and Morals* (New York: Dover Publications, Inc., 1961); Lagler, Bardach, Miller, Passino, *Ichthyology 2nd Edition* (New York: John Wiley & Sons, 1977); J.R. Norman, *A History of Fishes* (London: Ernest Benn Limited, 1975: (Third Edition by P.H. Greenwood); Gunther Sterba, *Freshwater Fishes of the World* (New York: The Pet Library, 1967); and Alwyne Wheeler, *Fishes of the World* (New York: Macmillan Publishing Co., Inc., 1975).

2. The material on mammals is developed from Everhard J. Slijper, *Whales and Dolphins* (Ann Arbor: The University of Michigan Press, 1977); John Farrand, Jr. *The Audubon Society Encyclopedia of Animal Life* (New York: Clarkson N. Potter, Inc. Distributed by Crown Publishers, Inc., 1982); Sir Richard Harrison and M.M. Bryden, *Whales, Dolphins, and Porpoises* (New York: Oxford, England: Facts on File Publications, 1988); Katona, Rough, Richardson, *A Field Guide to the Whales, Porpoises, and Seals of the Gulf of Maine and Eastern Canada* (New York: Charles Scribner's Sons, 1983); Kenneth Mallory and Andrea Conley, *Rescue of the Stranded Whales* (New York: Simon and Schuster, 1989); and L. Harrison Matthews, *The Natural History of the Whale,* (New York, Columbia University Press, 1978).

3. Notes about the conservation of aquatic animals are taken from J. Cousteau and staff of the Cousteau Society, *The Cousteau Almanac* (New York: Doubleday & Company, Inc., 1981); Lee Durrell, *State of the Ark* (New York: Doubleday and Company, Inc., 1986); and Les Kaufman and Kenneth Mallory, *The Last Extinction* (Cambridge, Massachusetts: London, England: The MIT Press, 1986).

4. The material on invertebrates is developed from Keith Banister and Andrew Campbell, *The Illustrated Encyclopedia of Aquatic Life* (New York: Facts on File, 1985); Peter Farb and the Editors of Life, *The Insects* (New York: Time Incorporated, 1962) 141–159; Kenneth Gosner, *A Field Guide to the Atlantic Seashore—The Peterson Guide Series* (Boston: Houghton Mifflin, 1978); B. Grzimek, *Grzimek's Animal Life Encyclopedia, Volume I, Lower Animals* (New York: Van Nostrand Reinhold Company, 1972) 142–3, 195–6; M. Jacobson and D. Franz. *Wonders of Corals and Coral Reefs* (New York: Dodd, Mead & Company, 1979) 14–38; Kaye Mash, *How Invertebrates Live* (London: Elsevier-Phaidon, 1975) 101–115; N. Meinkoth. *The Audubon Society Field Guide to North American Seashore Creatures* (New York: Alfred A. Knopf, 1981); Lorus and Margery Milne, *Invertebrates of North America* (New York: Doubleday and Company, Inc.); A. Ross and W. Emerson, *Wonders of Barnacles* (New York: Dodd, Mead & Company, 1974); 18–21, 22–37; T.E. Thompson, *Nudibranchs* (Neptune, N.J.: T.F.H. Publications, Inc., LTD., 1976) 79–86; and Warren Zeiller, *Tropical Marine Invertebrates of Southern Florida and the Bahama Islands* (New York: John Wiley and Sons, 1974) 26.

5. The material on birds is developed from B. Grzimek, *Grzimek's Animal Life Encyclopedia, Volume 8 Birds II* (New York: Van Nostrand Reinhold Company, 1975), 144–6; and G. Simpson, *Penguins: Past and Present, Here and There* (New Haven and London: Yale University Press, 1976) 77–117.

Suggested Reading

Bailey, Jill. *Fish.* New York: Facts On File, 1990.

Baker, Jeannie. *Where the Forest Meets the Sea.* New York: Greenwillow Books, 1987.

Bender, Lionel. *Fish to Reptiles.* New York: Franklin Watts, 1988.

Brewster, Bernice. *Discovering Freshwater Fish.* Janet Caulkins ed. New York: Franklin Watts, 1988.

Jacobson, Morris, and David Franz. *Wonders of Corals and Coral Reefs.* New York: Dodd, Mead, and Company, 1979.

Mallory, Kenneth, and Andrea Conley. *Rescue of the Stranded Whales.* New York: Simon and Schuster, 1989.

McGovern, Ann. *Shark Lady—True Adventures of Eugenie Clark.* New York: Scholastic Book Services, 1978.

Parker, Steve. *Fish: Eyewitness Books.* New York: Alfred A. Knopf, 1990.

Parker, Steve. *Pond and River: Eyewitness Books.* New York: Alfred A. Knopf, 1988.

Patent, Dorothy Hinshaw. *Dolphins and Porpoises.* New York: Holiday House, 1987.

Patent, Dorothy Hinshaw. *Fish and How They Reproduce.* New York: Holiday House, 1976.

Peterson, Roger Tory. *Penguins.* Boston: Houghton Mifflin Company, 1979.

Quinn, Kay. *A Look at Fish.* Los Angeles: Price Stern Sloan, Inc., 1986.

Ranger Rick. *Amazing Creatures of the Sea.* Washington: National Wildlife Federation, 1987.

Ranger Rick. *Endangered Animals.* Washington: National Wildlife Federation, 1989.

Reed, Don C. *Sevengill: The Shark and Me.* New York: Knopf, 1986.

Ross, Arnold, and William K. Emerson. *Wonders of Barnacles.* New York: Dodd, Mead, and Company, 1974.

Segaloff, Nat, and Paul Erickson. *Fish Tales.* New York: Sterling Publishing Company, Inc., 1990.

Sharp, David. *Animal Days: Animals from the Rivers and Oceans.* Sydney, Australia: Bay Books, distributed by Salem House, 1984.

Stevens, John. *Sharks.* New York: Facts On File, 1987.

Stone, Lynn M. *The Penguins.* Mankato, Minn.: Mankato, 1987.

Wheeler, Alwyne. *Discovering Saltwater Fish.* New York: Franklin Watts, 1988.

Index

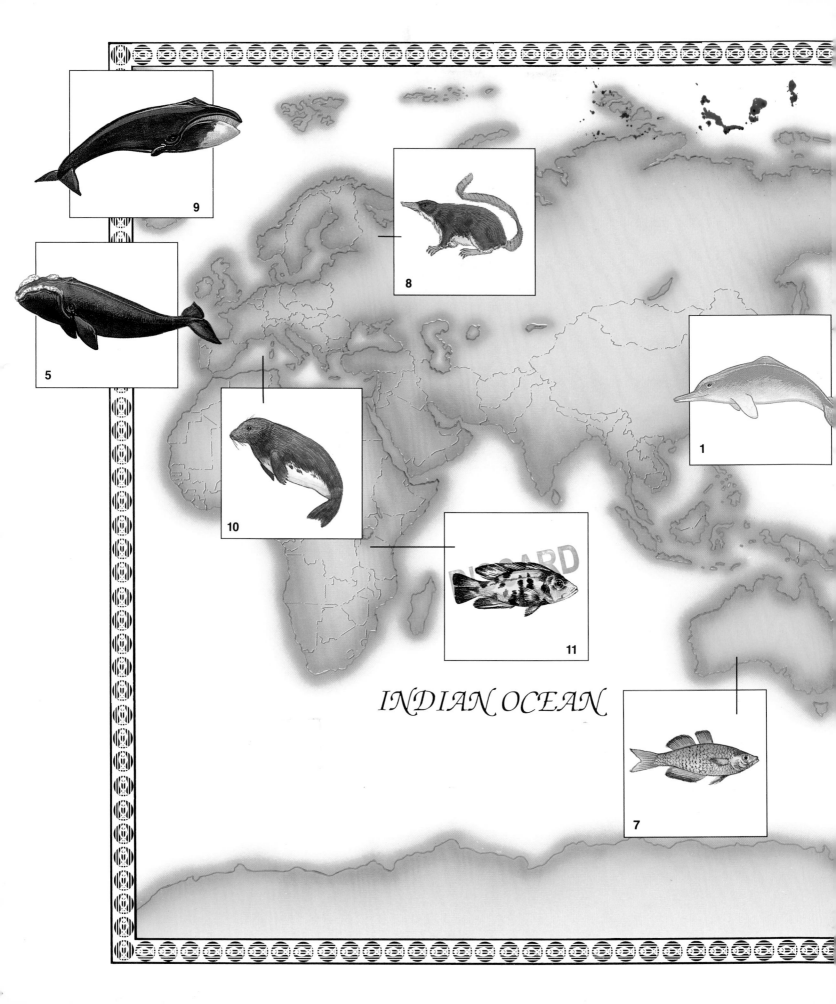

9

5

8

1

10

11

INDIAN OCEAN

7